GURU ANGAD DEV JEE, MY NANA JEE AND ME

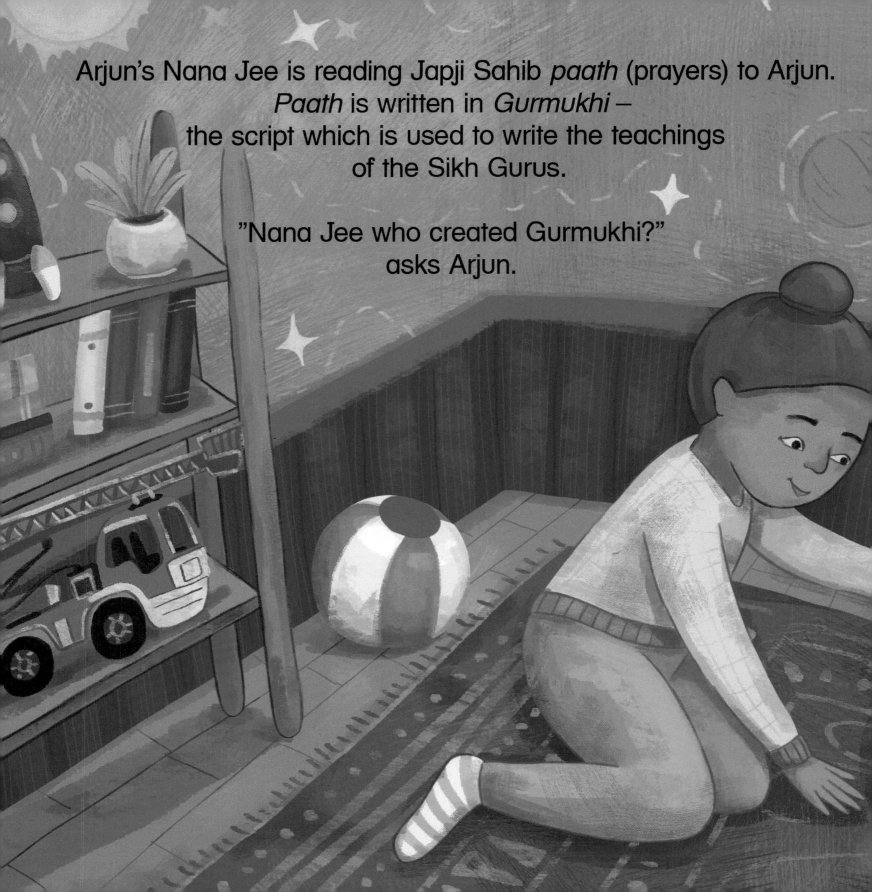

Arjun's Nana Jee is reading Japji Sahib *paath* (prayers) to Arjun.
Paath is written in *Gurmukhi* –
the script which is used to write the teachings
of the Sikh Gurus.

"Nana Jee who created Gurmukhi?"
asks Arjun.

Arjun's Nana Jee smiles at Arjun's curiosity and tells him that it comes from the Sikh's second Guru, Guru Angad Dev Jee.

Guru Angad Dev Jee was born in 1504 in *Sri Muktsar Sahib* in India. Guru Jee taught Punjabi and Gurmukhi to children. This helped them to understand *Gurbani* and *Waheguru Jee's* message to feel peace and to be successful in life.

Arjun loves to hear the meanings of Gurbani
from his Nana Jee when they do paath together.

Guru Angad Dev Jee said that
we should always remember Waheguru Jee
so we have good thoughts and make
good choices in life. Guru Angad Dev Jee taught us
that we should always follow our beliefs.

Arjun is very proud of his long hair
which is known as *kes*.

Once, a boy teased Arjun
about his long hair.
Arjun remembered Guru Jee's
message and told the boy
that he is a strong Sikh boy
and that his hair is his crown.

Although Arjun felt
a little sad
that the boy was unkind,
he knew we must
always be kind.

Echoing Guru Nanak Dev Jee's message,
Guru Angad Dev Jee believed in earning an honest living
and sharing. Guru Jee earned his living by twisting grass
in to strings used for cots. The money
that Guru Jee earnt while working was donated
to help the community. This is known as *seva* or charity.

Arjun likes to help others. As well as becoming a fireman when older, Arjun would like to become a teacher to teach children like his little brother Saajan who has Down's syndrome. People with Down's syndrome are just like you and me, they just take a little bit longer to learn. Arjun also likes to help with seva (selfless service) at the *Gurdwara*.

As well as hard work, Guru Jee took a keen interest in physical fitness and encouraged everyone to take part in sports and exercise. Guru Jee provided opportunities to everyone regardless of their religion, background or ability to take part in sports.

Arjun and Saajan love to play wrestling together!

It was very important to Guru Angad Dev Jee that men and women were treated equally as we are all equal in God's eyes. Guru Angad Dev Jee recognised the important things that women could contribute and that men could contribute.

Jovan is good at gardening

Evie Rose is good at running

Guru Jee practised equality by working with his wife, *Mata Khivi Jee*, to establish a free community kitchen where everybody is welcome. Men and women all sit together in a row, regardless of caste or status, ability and eat the same food. This is known as *langar*.

Arjun and Saajan's favourite
place to eat is at the Gurdwara
where they get to enjoy yummy *kheer*!

Kheer was something that
Mata Khivi Jee used to make.
By thinking of others, Guru Jee and Mata Khivi Jee showed
kindness, respect and have bought happiness to others.

Mata Khivi Jee and Guru Angad Dev Jee made food with love and care for healthy, nutritious and wholesome eating. It was very important to Guru Jee that we take care of our physical health.

Arjun and Saajan love to eat treats
but also ensure they have their fruit and vegetables!
Arjun enjoys learning about healthier choices
and his favourites are cucumbers and sweetcorn!
Saajan's are bananas and asparagus!

Guru Angad Dev Jee taught us the importance of making
the right choices by always remembering Waheguru Jee,
sharing with others equally and taking care of our health
by eating yummy nutritious food as well as exercising.

Guru Jee said that being a good person who did good actions,
doing our paath and meditating
would bring us closer to Waheguru Jee and bring us peace.